A Simplified Tax Structure for

The United States

M.S. Platt, J.D.

This book was printed in the United States of America.

To order additional copies of this book, contact Amazon.com. An inexpensive e-book version of this document is available from Amazon.com.

Table of Contents

The Purpose of This Publication

One may rightfully ask, "Why take the time and trouble to write about tax reform?" The answer is simple. As noted in the first citation of this publication, many people lament about the tax code, but Congress has done nothing to change it. Politicians offer many proposals, but Congress has yet to enact any legislation. The reason is that too many interests are involved, and not all can be satisfied. The author attempts to deal with this conundrum. He offers a tax structure that should satisfy most of the people who are engaged in politics in this country. Above all, he presents a tax plan that is fair to the poor as well as the wealthy. The author shows that no one really needs to pay high taxes. In fact, the suggested plan can be used to avoid high taxes and the complexities of the present code. It is simple to administer.

The author desires to share his ideas by submitting this publication. Inexpensive e-book and print versions are available. He hopes that the people in this country will read them and seriously consider adopting many of the suggestions that are made.

Marvin S. Platt
August 2015

A Simplified Tax Structure for the United States

There has been considerable controversy concerning Title 26 of the United States Tax Code. As noted in the first citation (1), multiple parties have lamented about its complexities and its length. In that citation, the Government Printing Office has reported that it is over 3500 pages long (perhaps 13,000 pages depending on the source) (1). Critics have complained that it is convoluted, cumbersome, costly, difficult to administer, and unfairly progressive to various economic classes (2). It favors special classes. It is used as a political instrument and occupies much time and effort by Congress. Yet in 2012, it generated approximately $ 2.5 trillion in revenue for this country (3). Thus, it is a major source of financial security for the nation. Most of the income is derived from individual and corporate taxes (3), and these are discussed in the proposal forwarded in this publication. In fact, any proposal should be compared to the present code. Thus, an analysis of the present individual and corporate tax codes is warranted. We first consider individual taxes.

A. The Tax Code for Individuals

One can easily analyze the individual tax code by referring to **Table 1.1** It is denominated as All Returns: Selected Income and Tax Items by Size and Accumulated Size of Adjusted Gross Income (AGI) (4). Obtain **Table 1.1** by using the pathway—Google > Size of Adjusted Gross Income >Individual Statistical Tables by Size, Publication 1304, 2012. The last available complete data were for 2012. Thus information for that year will be analyzed and discussed. An overview of **Table 1.1** shows some important heading columns. These are: Size of AGI by Income; Number of Returns; AGI, less deficit; Taxable Income (TI); Revenue Income. All the values are reported in millions for the number of returns and billions for the dollar amounts. If one examines **Table 1.1**, one finds that the total number of returns for 2012 was 144.9 million and the total AGI was $ 9,100 billion. AGI is the approximate income of an individual tax bracket and is gathered from aggregate information listed on the bottom line of the first page of Form 1040. The taxable income (TI) is the dollar amount of groups or any individual after all the deductions and exemptions are subtracted from the AGI. This is the amount that is subject to taxation. The revenue is the amount that the government collects. The effective tax is the real percentage by which individuals are taxed. The following example will clarify these notions.

A lawyer earns $60,000 from various sources in 2012 and reports it on the last line on Form 1040. He has expenses and state property tax and donation deductions of $10,000 in pursuing his practice. He has a personal exemption of $3800.

He can then deduct $13,800 from $60,000. The remainder, $46,200, is his taxable income. His effective tax is about 13%. It is not his marginal tax of 25%. This concept is explained below.

Referring to **Table 1.1** for 2012, the following information for the various income brackets becomes evident. These are shown in **Exhibit A**.

Exhibit A

Income Bracket	# Returns (millions)	AGI (billions.........billions)	TI	Revenue	Eff Tax %
0-$20,000	48.6	285.0	61.0	6.1	9.9
20-$40,000	33.3	970.2	347.3	39.3	11.3
40-$100,000	41.8	2,701.6	1709.3	222.5	13.0
100-$200,000	15.6	2,101.0	1,563.0	265.4	17.0
200-$500,000	4.5	1,186.7	957.0	231.6	24.2
Over $500,000	1.09	1,858.0	1,607.1	422.9	26.3
TOTALS	144.9	9,100	6,246	1,188	

The information obtained from **Exhibit A** and **Table 1.1** is quite interesting. It shows that the effective tax, the ratio of revenue to taxable income, varies from 9.9 to 26.3 %. Note that the effective tax rate is the amount that each individual filer actually pays. It is distinct from the marginal tax rate for tax filers. The marginal tax is distinctly **not** the tax that anyone pays. The marginal tax brackets reported by the Internal Revenue Service for 2012 (IRS Tax Schedules) for single filers were as follows:

Marginal Tax, 2012 (single filers used as base for comparison)

10% for taxable incomes	$0-$8700
15% for taxable incomes.......	$8700-$35,350
25% for taxable incomes........	$35,350-$85,650
28% for taxable incomes	$85,650- $178,650
33% for taxable incomes........	$178,650- $388,350
35% for taxable incomes.......	Over $388,350

Note that there were 6 brackets in 2012. In 2015, there were 7 brackets. The added bracket was at a marginal rate of 39.6% for a taxable income of over $464,850.

From information in **Exhibit A** and **Table 1.1**, one can calculate the approximate amount of the total deductions for each bracket. This amount is obtained by subtracting the TI (in billions) from the AGI (in billions) for each bracket. Then divide this amount by the number (#) of returns.

This process will give the approximate total deduction (in thousands) for each bracket as:

0-$20,000..................	$285.0-$61.0/48.6= $4,610
20-$40,000................	$970.2-$347.3/33.3= $18,710
40-$100,000..............	$2701.6-$1709.3= $23,740
$100-$200,000...........	$2,101-$1563/15.6= $34,490
$200,000-$500,000...	$1,106.7-$957= $55,349
Over $500,000............	$230,280

Note that for the first three tax brackets, individuals reduce their AGI by about $20,000 or less, whereas the higher income individuals reduce their taxes by maximizing their deductions or using lower long-term capital gains rates. However, even though they take higher deductions, they pay no more than 24.2 to 26.3% effective taxes (see **Exhibit A**). Thus, the tax code could be simplified easily by reducing the tax rates and allowing a single deduction.

Wealthy individuals could still purchase or donate items but need not use them as deductions. A donor need not be motivated by a tax deduction, but be motivated by one's benevolent intent.

A similar analysis was applied to **Table 1.1** for 2008 and gave the same results. Thus, an early recession year (2008) did not show different results than a post recession year (2012).

The wealthy maintain that they carry a significant proportion of the tax burden. Indeed, they do. For example, the higher tax bracket individuals (those with an AGI greater than $200,000 per year) submit approximately 55.1% of the total revenue. This value is obtained by using the data from **Table 1.1** and **Exhibit A**. The value 55.1% is obtained by calculating as follows: Take the TI of the bracket, divide by the total revenue, and multiply by 100; or $654.5/$1,188 (in billions) x 100= 55.1%. Therefore, the wealthy account for 55.1% of revenue, but they constitute only about 4% of the 144.9 million tax returns (from **Table 1.1**).

However, the wealthy must realize that without their contribution, the poor and middle classes would not be able to work, purchase goods and services, contribute maximally to the economy and defense of this country and maintain the economy such that the wealthy can obtain incomes to prosper. Thus, this country needs the wealthy as well as the poor and the middle classes. Each contributes to the operations of the country. That is what makes this country and economy function. That is what motivates the poor to improve their economic status and become wealthy. That is the dream of our capitalistic society. One social group relies on the other. It is the *"yin/yang"* of our culture. THIS COUNTRY DOES NOT NEED CLASS WARFARE. IT NEEDS CLASS COOPERATION.

Given the economic and philosophical approaches presented here, what kind of simplified tax code for individuals is suggested?

The following tax schedule's elements and attributes are as follows:

1. There will be four tax brackets for TI (6, 12, 18, 24-28%).
2. A single maximum deduction of $20,000 applies to each taxpayer.
3. Single, working or non-working married or civil- union couples, heads of households, working cohabitating parties would file separately. Each individual would obtain a $20,000 single deduction. Since approximately 60% of couples work (5), individuals of many working cohabitating couples would deduct $20,000 separately from their AGI. However, married and civil-union couples, and head of household families would be allowed to deduct $40,000 to allow for family and childhood expenses.
4. Since the lesser income parties would deduct $20,000 or more annually (as shown in 3 above), families with children who deduct $20,000 to $40,000 would pay no taxes.

5. The wealthy would still only pay an effective tax rate of 24-26% (see **Exhibit** A). Assuming that the 2015 long-term capital gains tax rate would remain the same and be no greater than 20% for the wealthy (6), a party making over $200,000 annually who invests at least half of his/her income would be taxed at 24-26%. This value is obtained by considering 28%+20%/2= 24% (highest tax rate+ capital gains rate/2). Lower income individuals would still use long-term capital gain rates (0 to 15%) similar to their present brackets as they do now (6).

6. The abuse of claiming inappropriate or fraudulent deductions would be eliminated. IRS audits would be minimalized. The IRS would shrink in size.

7. The cost and administration of this schedule would be markedly decreased. The calculations would be simple. The paper load would be reduced.

8. It would be fair to all classes.

9. It would motivate investment and savings.

10. It would reduce the national debt because more revenue would be obtained (see below), and the wealthy would be motivated to invest in Treasury Notes and Bonds.

11. Since the wealthy are not taxed more, they would have more funds to invest.

An example of this proposed tax schedule is presented in **Exhibit B**.

Exhibit B (bracket x1000, returns in millions, AGI to Revenue in billions, rates in %)

Bracket	Tax	# returns	AGI	Deduction	TI	Revenue	Eff rate
0-20	6	48.6	285	970	0	0	0
20-40	6	33.3	970.2	667	303.2	18.2	6
40-100	12	41.8	2,701.6	836	1,862.5	223.5	12
100-200	18	15.6	2,101.0	312	1,787.1	321.7	18
200-500	28*	4.15	1,186.7	83	1,103.7	286.9	26
Over 500	28*	1.09	1,858.0	21.8	1,836.0	477.4	26
TOTALS		144.9	9,101.0	2,890	6,892.6	1,327.7	

The average tax for all returns would be 19% (1,327/6,892 x 100= 19%.) *Taxpayers earning greater than $200,000 would not be taxed at 28% but at 24-26% as noted above.

To show how this new tax structure would operate, several examples are presented.
1. The poor with incomes of less than $20,000 annually would not pay any federal taxes.
2. For the $20,000 -$40,000 taxable income bracket, the total deduction for the 33.3 million filers would be 33.3 million x $20,000, a deduction equal to $667.0 billion. The taxable income for this group would be $970.2 (AGI) minus $667.0 or $ $303.2 billion. The tax would be 6% of $303.2 billion or $18.2 billion in revenue. The effective tax rate would be 6%, calculated from Revenue/TI x 100 ($18.2/303.2 x 100 =6%).

3. Using this same mathematical approach, the revenues and effective tax rates would be, as shown in **Exhibit B**, as 6, 12,18, 26%. Taxpayers in the $100-$200,000 TI range could lower their 18% rate to 16% by investing and using their lower long-term rates (6) of 15% (18+15/2=16.5).

4. The total revenue would be $1,327 billion ($1.327 trillion). The actual revenue in 2012 was $1,188 billion. Thus, $139 billion more would be achieved.

5. The effective tax rate for the wealthy would remain at 24% -26% (compare **Exhibits A and B**).

6. Business owners and corporations would be taxed at lower rates of 24% or less (rates appropriate for their income). See the corporation taxation discussion below.

7. In time of war or national emergencies, an across the board increase of these rates could be voted by Congress. A 1% increase of these rates would yield approximately $150 billion more in revenue. Higher rate increases may be necessary in certain circumstances.

Other tax plans have been proposed (7). A single "flat" tax of either 17% or 21% on taxable income does not generate sufficient revenue; e.g., a 17% tax on a TI of $6892 billion would maximally yield $1,172 billion, but it would be unfair to poor taxpayers. If some of the poor were excluded from taxation, less revenue would be obtained. Those taxpayers who have effective tax rates of 13 to 17% would be penalized since a TI of $40,000 to $100,000 would be taxed at greater than 12%. Another proposal, the "fair tax," is a sales tax. It is estimated that the tax would be as high as 10% or more. Even if the poor receive rebates, it taxes them unfairly. In addition, it plagued by fraud and poor management.

Several proposals (8) modify or erase deductions but do not satisfy real estate or other interests. The present proposal does not discriminate against any interests. It allows families to use their $20,000 to $40,000 deduction at their own discretion; e.g., mortgage payments, donations to religious groups and other charitable institutions, etc. Families would not even need to list the deductions. This proposal does limit deductions by the wealthy, but these groups would still have lower tax rates of 24-26%. They would then have ample remaining funds to purchase whatever they desired, and they would not need to use quasi-legal modalities to claim these deductions from the Internal Revenue Service.

B. The Tax Code for Corporations

The status of corporate taxation in the United States is also controversial. Although there is a great deal wrong with the nation's corporate tax code (9), corporate taxation will not "go away" because the federal government obtains approximately 10% of its annual income from this source. This revenue of $267 billion is 10% of the nation's total income of $2,455 billion (10).

The corporate tax code needs improvement, but we cannot change it until we gain insight into its problems. Many, but not all, of the problems are cited below.

1. First, one must define the term corporation as addressed in the code. A corporation as defined in Merriam-Webster's dictionary is "an organization that under the law has the rights and duties of an individual and follows

a specific purpose." Corporations usually attain this status by applying for and obtaining a state charter that specifies the rights, duties and purpose of this legal entity. One must differentiate C corporations from S corporations. S corporations are smaller businesses that have single taxation; that is, their profits or losses are passed directly to the shareholders who own the corporation. These persons pay a single tax. C corporations are larger businesses with many shareholders who are the owners, but these corporations have double taxation. The businesses pay a corporate tax, and the shareholders pay individual taxes on the dividends they receive from the business. In most circumstances, the shareholders in both entities cannot be held liable for any fiscal obligations or legal malfeasances. C corporations are the entities that the Internal Revenue corporation tax governs, and these will be addressed in the present discussion. Partnerships and S corporations are "pass –through" entities; their profits are taxed singularly and directly to the partners or shareholders respectively. They pay the individual tax rates. Two well-written resources from the Congressional Research Service of the Library of Congress provide valuable insights into the problems that corporations face (12,13).

2. The U. S. corporate tax rate varies from 15% to 39% (11). Corporations with less than $75,000 annual taxable income pay 15-25%. Taxable income for a corporation is the total income minus the cost of goods and services, and multiple deductions, exemptions, and credits (13).

Corporations with taxable incomes above $100,000 annually are subject to a 34 - 39% tax (11). Many large corporations in the United States are multinational and operate throughout the world. They are frequently referred to as Standard and Poor 500 or Fortune 500 entities.

3. The United States uses a worldwide corporate tax system (12, 13). This system taxes all the income that a corporation earns throughout the world. However, multinational corporations can "defer" income derived outside of the U.S. (12). They are subject to all their taxable income if they return their foreign income to themselves or shareholders in the U. S. (12). However, many reinvest their foreign profits in lower tax foreign nations and pay lower taxes (12). The U.S. retrieved approximately $312 billion of this "off-shore" profit during a "tax holiday" in 2004, but large amounts were still kept from the U. S. Treasury (14). In addition, the worldwide system allows multinational corporations to claim a tax credit for taxes paid to foreign nations (12, 13).

In contrast to a worldwide system, a territorial tax system (12, 13) is popular in European and Asian nations. This system taxes corporations mainly for income derived within a national border. In truth, worldwide or territorial systems do not exist in pure form. Each has some exceptions and variations and, therefore, is a hybrid (12, 13). The territorial system allows domestic corporations to compete in foreign markets since they pay lower taxes in these markets (12, 13). Unfortunately, this system may motivate U. S. corporations to invest in low tax countries and hire foreign workers—a detriment to the U. S. economy.

4. Given these facts, it becomes evident that the corporate tax code is quite complicated. It has too many credits and deductions, and it tends to benefit certain taxpayers and harm others. It causes corporations and shareholders to be subject to "double taxation" (12, 13). This phenomenon occurs in two circumstances. First, U. S. corporations are subject to U. S. taxes and foreign nation taxes. Tax credits in the tax code tend to ameliorate this dilemma. The other circumstance is when U. S. corporations and shareholders pay double taxes to the U. S. government. Corporations pay the corporate tax; shareholders pay individual taxes on the income derived from dividends paid to them from the corporation.

5. The revenue derived from the corporate tax code is decreasing (13). This is, in part, related to the recent recession. However, it is also due to the fact that corporations are moving to other countries and use multiple accounting procedures to decrease taxable income. In addition, smaller companies are moving to "pass-through" entities so as to avoid double taxation. They take advantage of the lower individual tax rates for these entities.

6. The United States has one of the highest corporate tax rates, 39%, of all the well-developed nations in the world (15). Commentators have argued that this is not true, but that corporations actually pay much less. They pay an effective rate of approximately 25% or less (16). An

effective tax rate is the rate that a corporation pays by reducing its taxable income and paying lower taxes.

7. Various strategies (13) have been suggested to improve the present corporate tax structure, but none have gained consensus or enactment by the Congress. Some of these suggestions, and rebuttals to them (13), show how complex the corporate tax problem is. Some of these unmet suggestions are as follows:

(a). Broaden the tax base and lower the rates. The National Commission on Fiscal Responsibility and Reform suggested this change in December 2010 (17). No one could agree on what expenditures to terminate, and the suggested 28% tax rate was considered too high and not workable (12, 13).

(b). Integrate the corporate and individual tax systems. A 1992 Treasury Report noted that this approach would decrease federal revenues (12). Congress could eliminate corporate taxes and allocate earnings directly to shareholders (12). However, this notion would raise multiple administrative and record-keeping issues (12).

(c). The United States could adopt some variation of a territorial system. This concept was defined above. Indeed, many European nations noted that a territorial system did not cause labor/employment issues and did not adversely affect revenue.

(d). Congress could modify the corporate tax so that revenues would be "revenue neutral" (13); that is, revenues would approximate what the Treasury presently receives. This change must be made carefully because "revenue neutrality" may place burdens on other taxpayers (13).

What revenues would Treasury receive if option 7(d), "tax neutrality, " were adopted? This information can be obtained easily by reviewing the Internal Revenue Service reports dealing with corporations. A search of SOI Tax Stats, Corporation Complete Report 2012 at Figure A, page 2 yields this important information (18) and addresses this search. The year 2012 was chosen because it gave the most recent available data. Several columns of data in this report are noteworthy. These columns are denominated as follows: number of returns, total receipts, net income, income subject to tax, total income tax *before* credits, total income tax *after* credits (i.e., the federal revenue). For 2012 and 2008, the following data are shown in **Exhibit C**. Note that the **TI** is the net income subject to tax *before* credits. The #returns are in millions; receipts, net income and **TI** in trillions; revenue in billions. The first line contains 2012 data. The second line contains 2008 data.

Exhibit C

# Returns	Total Receipts	Net Income	TI	Revenue
5.8	29.4	1.774	1.149	267.8
5.8	28.6	0.9843	0.9781	228.6

If a territorial system were adopted, the issues of foreign tax credits, deferred income, and tax holidays would be mainly resolved. Thus, the column denominated income subject to tax *after* credits is not needed or shown in **Exhibit C**. In 2012, the effective tax rate was 267.8/1,149 (in billions) x100 =23%, derived from revenue/TI x 100. In 2008, the effective tax rate was 228.6/978.1 (in billions) x 100=23%. Both were the same, notwithstanding the fact that these years were before and after the recession.

Therefore, the United States can lower its corporate tax rate from 39% to 24%, adopt a territorial system, and avoid dealing with foreign tax credits and deferred income and still be revenue neutral. Corporations could still deduct the cost of goods and services and various deductions that S corporations and partnerships presently do.

THIS IS THE CONCEPT THAT IS RECOMMENDED AS THE CORPORATE TAX IN THIS PUBLICATION. A territorial system with a corporate tax rate of 24% is suggested for corporations with taxable incomes greater than $200,000. Corporations with taxable incomes less than $200,000 would pay at the individual tax rates assigned to S corporations and partnerships. A tax of 24% for larger corporations would be close to the capital gains and effective tax rates recommended for wealthy individual, partnership, and S corporation taxpayers (see Section A above). This tax structure would unify the corporate and individual tax systems. It would be competitive with most of the developed nations in the world (15). It would avoid many of the complications and complexities of the present U. S. worldwide system. It would be revenue neutral.

This plan would yield approximately $275.7 billion in revenue, derived from $1,149 (billions)(the **TI**) x 24% = $275.7 billion. The revenue received by the Treasury in 2012 was approximately $267.8 billion (18). Thus, the recommended plan would be tax neutral for 2012.

C. Other tax revenues.

Social security/payroll, excise, custom duty and estate/gift taxes constitute other sources of revenue for the federal government. The excise, custom duty, and estate/gift taxes accounted for only 3%, 1.1%, and 0.68% of revenue respectively in 2012(19). The estate and gift taxes now allow an exemption of $5.43 million for a donor (20). Therefore, these revenue sources are not presently at issue.

D. Conclusion

Title 26 of the United States tax code needs revision. The individual and corporate codes are lengthy, cumbersome, complex, and unfair to various constituents of our society. This publication reviews the areas of complexity and offers simplified, easily executed procedures to replace these two segments of the tax code. Any discussions dealing with a better health care system, Medicare, the social security system and payroll taxes, and the national debt should be addressed in a separate publication.

E. Citations

1. What is The Real Size of the U. S. Federal Tax Code. The Isaac Brock Society. February 12, 2012. Quote of U. S. Government Printing Office, page 4 of 18. Retrieved August 4, 2015.
2. Wood RW. 20 Really Stupid Things in the U. S. Tax Code. Forbes, December 16, 2014. Retrieved August 1, 2015.
3. IRS Releases FY 2012 Data Book. March 25, 2013. U. S. Government Printing Office. Retrieved August 1, 2015.
4. 2012 Federal Income Tax Brackets (IRS Tax Rates). Forbes, September 30, 2011. Retrieved July 30, 2015.
5. Bureau of Labor Statistics, U. S. Department of Labor, The Economics Daily, Employment characteristics of families, 2012. Retrieved August 1, 2015.
6. Taxes: What's New for 2015? -Charles Schwab. January 4, 2015, page 1 of 4. Retrieved August 4, 2015.
7. The Tax Code: Make It Flat. Forbes, March 7,2014, page 1 of 6. Retrieved August 4, 2014.
8. The Moment of Truth-National Commission on Fiscal Responsibility and Reform, December 2010, pp. 28-31. Retrieved August 3, 2015.
9. McBride W. Beyond the Headlines: What Do Corporations Pay in Income Tax? Tax Foundation, September 2011, pp. 1-2. Retrieved August 4, 2015.
10. The Budget and Economic Outlook: Fiscal Years 2013-2023. Congressional. Budget Office, February 5, 2013.Table 1.1, p .9. Retrieved August 4, 2015.
11. Corporate Tax Rate Schedule, 2014. Tax Policy Center. April 11,2014. Retrieved July 30, 2015.

12. Keightley MP, Stupak JM. U. S. International Corporate
    Taxation: Basic Concepts and Policy Issues.
    Congressional Research Service, December 2,
    2014. Retrieved August 5, 2015.

13. Keightley MP, Sherlock MF. The Corporate Income
    System: Overview and Options for Reform.
    Congressional Research Service, December 1, 2014.
    Retrieved August 6, 2015.

14. Peterson, K. Report: Repatriation Tax Holiday a
    "Failed" Policy. The Wall Street Journal. October 10,
    2011. Retrieved August 7, 2015.

15. Pomerleau, K. Corporate Income Tax Rates Around
    the World, 2014. Tax Foundation. August 20, 2014.
    Retrieved August 5, 2015.

16. Worstall, T. U.S. Corporations Only Paid 13% of Their
    Profits in Federal Tax: Apple is the Explanation for
    This. Forbes. July 3, 2013. Retrieved August 5, 2015.

17. The Moment of Truth- National Commission on Fiscal
    Responsibility and Reform. December 2010.
    pp. 32-33. Retrieved August 3, 2015.

18. SOI Tax Stats-Corporation Complete Report, 2008
    and 2012. IRS. Retrieved August 6, 2015.

19. Where Will Federal Revenue Come from in 2014?
    http://taxfoundation.org/blog/where-will-federal-
    tax-revenue-come-2014. October 25, 2013. Retrieved
    August 6, 2015.

20. Ebeling A. IRS Announces 2015 Estate and Gift
    Tax Limits. Forbes. October 30, 2014.
    Retrieved August 7, 2015.

Acknowledgement

I wish to thank Anna Maria Barnum for advising me during the production of this publication.

Other Publications of Monte Verde Press (also available from Amazon):

"Do Not Forsake Me ," Martin Luther King, Jr. –The
  Uncertainty of His American Dream.
  (2007 and 2012).

  Holy Economics - Resolving the Debt Crisis.
  (2011).

  Minyan: Ten Stories. (2008).

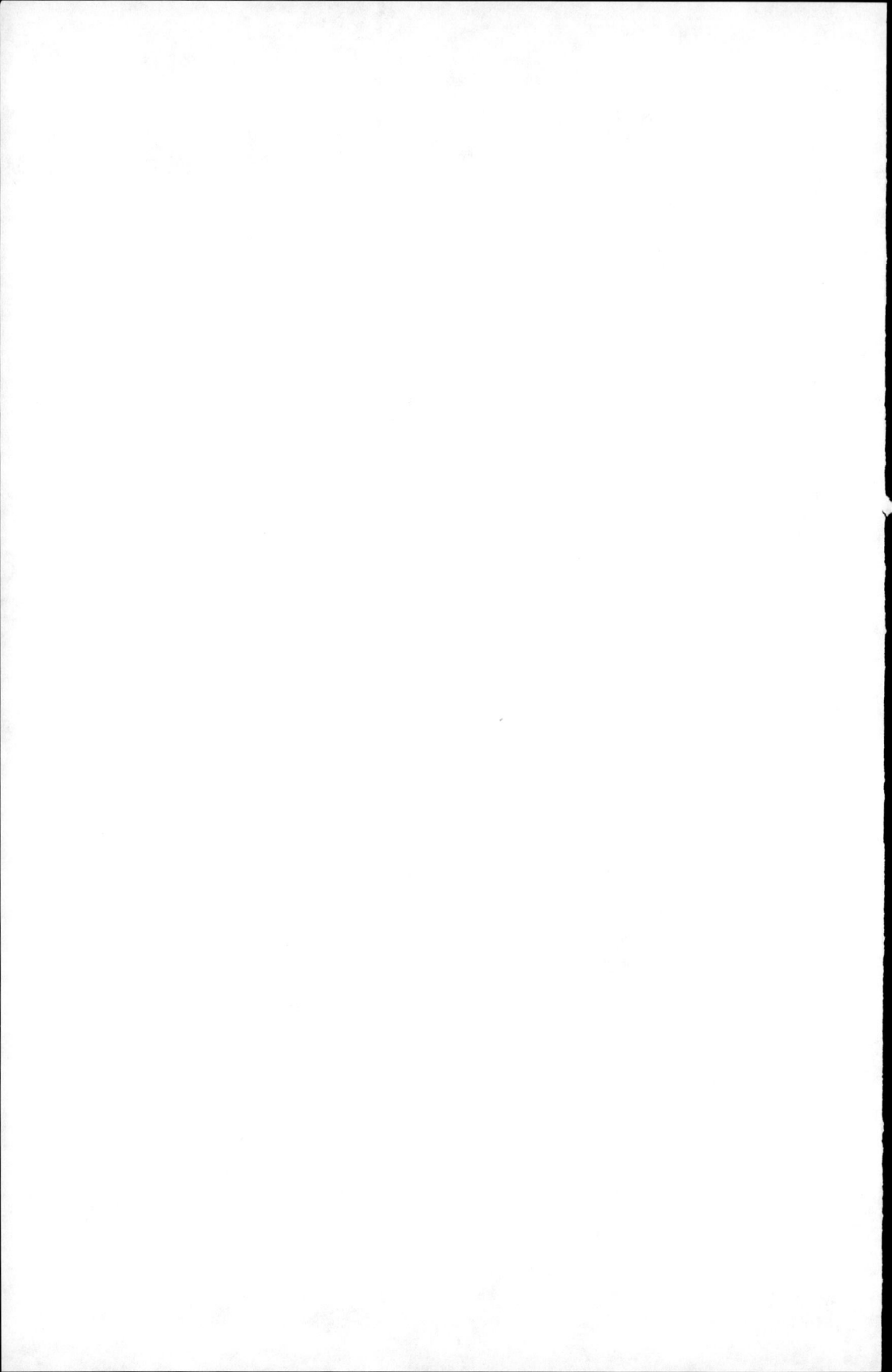

www.ingramcontent.com/pod-product-compliance
Lightning Source LLC
Chambersburg PA
CBHW032258210326
41520CB00048B/5516